KINGDOM PRAYER

To Sister Smith!
May Exploits of Prayer
& Breakthrough be your portion.

Apostle Stephen A. Garner

Rivers Publishing Company
Phone 773.826.1442
P.O. Box 528142, Chicago, IL 60652
E-mail: rolw@sbcglobal.net

ISBN - 978-0-9860068-0-7

Printed in the United States of America

Kingdom Prayer was written with the intent of helping believer's partner with Christ, through prayer, for the extension of His Kingdom. Each generation of believers, since the Lord's physical presence on the planet, have been entrusted with the responsibility of manifesting His Rule. The Lord states in Luke 11:2 we're to pray for His Kingdom to come and His will to be done as it is in heaven, so in the earth. The will of our King breaking into the earth is connected to prayer. This does not mean any kind of prayer but prayer that is inspired by our King. His will is rooted in His Kingdom manifesting in the earth. This manifestation will be visible among His people, though His Kingdom is a spiritual Kingdom and it belongs to those who are born of His Spirit.

Many believers who desire change and find it difficult to achieve should not fret nor be dismayed anymore, for the Kingdom of GOD is here. Matthew 11:1-5 gives an account of when John the Baptist was cast into prison and begins to question whether Jesus was the King or should they, John and his disciples, look for another. The Lord replies, *"the blind receive their sight, the lame walk, the lepers are cleansed, the death hear, the dead are raised and the poor have the gospel preached to them" (Matthew 11:5).* Signs like these had not taken place in all of humanity until Christ. The King of kings was among men fulfilling prophecy after prophecy concerning His rule on earth. You and I are now called to join in this blessed work and continue it in our generation. *"How great are His signs and how mighty are His wonders, His kingdom is an everlasting kingdom and His dominion is from generation to generation"* *(Daniel 4:3)*

The Kingdom of GOD is nothing new; it is an entity older than time itself. As a matter of fact, it has always existed. This is because its KING is eternal and HE is called the Ancient of Days, (Daniel 7:9, 13, 22). The Kingdom of GOD is an extension of an actual spiritual locale called the Kingdom of Heaven. This is important to know because the Kingdom of GOD is not a place. No GPS system or map can locate it. The natural eye cannot see it, nor can it be discerned through the natural senses. JESUS, the King of the kingdom, stated in the gospel of Luke 17:20, *"...the kingdom of GOD cometh not with observation..."* This is because the Kingdom of GOD is hidden within the heart of the born again believer.

Now, many of you are probably asking the question; "What is the Kingdom of GOD?" There are five words in the bible that are used for kingdom, however, for this book we will focus our attention on two: Strong's Hebrew Dictionary key 4438, *malkuyah*, and Greek Dictionary key 932, *basileia*. The Hebrew word *malkuyah* means rule, dominion, realm, reign, empire and kingdom. The meaning of the Greek word *basileia* is almost completely identical to its Hebrew counterpart. It means royalty, rule, realm, kingdom or reign. Based on these two words we can conclude that the Kingdom of GOD is the realm, rule, reign and dominion of GOD. Wherever this is manifested, there is the Kingdom of GOD. Every human being that was ever born was intended to live in this kingdom. As a matter of fact, the entire Earth was designed to be governed by this kingdom. Unfortunately, due to sin, the only place where this kingdom governs currently is the Ecclesia. That is the universal church, the called out body of Christ.

The body of Christ, or the church, is the entity where the Kingdom of GOD reigns. Therefore, as born again believers and members of Christ's many membered-body, we have been given the assignment of extending GOD's kingdom in the Earth. Over the years, the church has attempted to accomplish this mandate through several different ways. Some of these include: passing out tracts, inviting people to church, bible bashing unbelievers, being harsh and critical of political leaders and even passing Blue Sunday laws (the shutting down of businesses) in times past. Unfortunately, none of this has had any lasting positive effect or impact.

Daniel 2:35 declares that the Kingdom of GOD will fill the whole earth. Revelations 11:15 states that, eventually, *"the kingdoms of this world are become the kingdoms of our LORD and of His Christ and He shall reign forever and ever".* However, it must be understood that just because this is the will of GOD, it will not happen simply because of osmosis. There is a part that you and I as believers have to play to bring the will of GOD to pass in the earth. The Apostle Paul stated in I Corinthians 3:9 that, *"we are laborers together with GOD..."* This is always how GOD intended to operate on planet earth. Psalms 115:16 states: *"The heaven, even the heavens, are the LORD's: but the earth hath HE given to the children of men."* GOD needs humans to come into compliance with HIS will so that HE can manifest it on the earth. The late 16th century reformer and founder of the Presbyterian Church, John Knox, is quoted saying that; "GOD does nothing on the earth but in answer to believing prayer." When GOD originally created man in the Garden of Eden, HE gave him dominion and authority over the entire earth, (Genesis 1:28). Unfortunately, when man sinned he gave that authority over to Satan. When the second Adam, Jesus came to the earth, HE reclaimed that authority, (Matthew 28:18). Now every born again believer in Christ has also been given authority according to, Luke 10:19 and Acts 1:8.

With this authority also comes responsibility. The church is now the steward of planet earth. As Adam was the keeper of the garden in the beginning, we are now the keepers or watchmen over the earth through Christ.

If society is destroyed by the powers of hell, it is our fault. If chaos runs rampant in our nations, it is an indicator that the church has not been faithful to her assignment. We cannot sit back and blame sinners or the government for the ills of our nations when we refuse to do our part. What is our part, you may ask? It is to pray. It is to make intercession.

In America, there's much talk about revival. It is one of the most favorite topics for many preachers today. We hold revival conferences, we march, we protest, we speak out against certain ills of society, yet we fail to see revival. Could the reason possibly be that we have neglected to heed the words of the LORD recorded in the gospel of Matthew 9:37-38? Jesus said, *"Then saith he unto his disciples, The harvest truly is plenteous, but the labourers are few; Pray ye therefore the Lord of the harvest, that he will send forth labourers into his harvest."*

I am certain that this is the main reason why we have not been effective in arresting the powers of darkness that have controlled our nation. Every great move of revival recorded in history was precipitated by prayer. This is the only way we can effectively release the kingdom. When the church begins to pray that sent ones will be released, who have been empowered by GOD to reach every people group known to man with the grace and power of the KING, then true revival will take place in our nation.

Kingdom Principle

1

Prayer helps to identify, separate and mobilize ministry gifts.

"As they ministered to the Lord, and fasted, the Holy Ghost said, Separate me Barnabas and Saul for the work whereunto I have called them. And when they had fasted and prayed and laid their hands on them, they sent them away." Acts 13:2-3 KJV

Through the corporate effort of ministering to the Lord and praying, the Antioch leaders were able to stay true to a pattern seen in Christ. They set aside time to seek God's wisdom concerning ministries gifts that were to be set apart and released to fulfill the great commission. (See Mark 3:13-15 and Luke 6:12-13).

Paul, who was called Saul, and Barnabas were identified, received an apostolic commissioning and sent to advance the kingdom. It's noteworthy to mention that when we find apostles, prophets and teachers doing what was established in the church of Antioch in our time, the same results are destined to occur. Ministry gifts will be identified, commissioned and sent to extend the rule of GOD's kingdom.

It's through a concentrated effort of leadership united in prayer that nations can shift; multitudes in dark places can have the Gospel of the Kingdom preached to them and thereby encounter the true and living GOD. The catalyst for greater works is through intercession.

Kingdom Principle

2

Prayer serves as the foundation to identify the proper people for ordination.

"And it came to pass in those days, that He went out into a mountain to pray, and continued all night in prayer to GOD. And when it was day, He called unto Him His disciples: and of them He chose twelve, whom He also named apostles."   Luke 6:12-13 KJV

There are many leaders and believers who have, at one point in their walk with the Lord, cried, "I want to be more like you Jesus" and that's an awesome desire. However, the pattern to become like Him is in word and deed. His deeds were demonstrated in the place of prayer. There were times when He prayed all night. This shows that quality in prayer is necessary for greater works. Ministry gifts desiring a higher calling must practice this pattern which is to withdraw from ministry as usually and spend quality time in pray, especially at night.

The impact of Him praying all night led to the identifying of men whom He would send as apostles to turn the world upside down and birth the Church of which He Himself is the Head. Sometimes people are empowered and set in positions of importance for kingdom advancement and no time has been spent praying, especially all night. This behavior could potentially create hindrances to advancement.

Prayerlessness has become such a danger for the church today. While competent people are operating in their respective offices as ministry gifts to a local church the potential for a disservice may continue if the pattern for prayer is not embraced.

Kingdom Principle

Prayer breaks the limitations of ministry gifts due to demonic territorial powers.

"Peter therefore was kept in prison: but Prayer was made without ceasing of the church unto GOD for him."

Acts 12:5 KJV

Peter, an apostle, represents the apostolic anointing in a territory locked in a place of confinement. Satan hates apostles and apostolic churches that are used by GOD to extend the Kingdom. He often seeks to limit the influence, growth and visibility of these kinds of churches. The context of the referenced verse was during a time of intense persecution of the early church. Herod was murdering the apostles and looking to displace pressure coming towards him politically because of the intense famine which had hit the land. After the death of the Apostle James, the Apostle Peter was apprehended and sentenced to death.

The church, however, stretched out in prayer and continued without ceasing, i.e. they prayed fervently. Their prayers became so intense, that a powerful angel was released from heaven to deliver Peter from prison, where he was under the watch of several teams of soldiers. The angel escorts him to the iron gates which led to the city. The iron gates opened to him of their own accord. What a powerful deliverance!!

I'm convinced that when the church begins to stretch out in corporate prayer and intercedes for GOD to deliver ministry gifts, especially apostles and prophets we will see an increase of the anointing. This will help us become more effective in dealing with limitations imposed against the church through religious, political or social entities. This will result also in increased angelic encounters in our cities. We will also begin to see the Kingdom of GOD extended with the judgments of GOD descending on the powers of darkness responsible for chaos and spiritual dullness in our regions.

I pray that today will be one filled with encounters from the Most High. I pray for your life of prayer to increase and intensify mightily. I decree iron gates which resist you in the place of influence, expansion and deliverance to open unto you in the name of Jesus! May angels be released on your behalf and apostolic grace to stretch out in your calling. I decree open heavens and breakthrough in abundance over your life.

Kingdom Principle

Prayer serves as the catalyst that releases salvation in the earth.

"But this man, because he continueth ever, hath an unchangeable priesthood. Wherefore he is able also to save them to the uttermost that come unto GOD by him, seeing he ever liveth to make intercession for them."

Hebrews 7:24-25 KJV

One of the eternal activities of our high priest is intercession. The work of redemption and judgment against the father of lies was consummated thousands of years ago through the work of the cross. Jesus made a public show of the powers of darkness that had interfered with the redemption of man and reinstated humanity to our rightful place with GOD.

It is finished and the victory has been won. Why is there still a need for the work of intercession in the earth today? This work is still necessary because it provides access for salvation to manifest in any region of the earth and in every generation. It also secures access for future generations to come to know Jesus Christ as their personal Lord and Saviour. (See Daniel 4:34 and Psalm 145:13)

May a divine allegiance be forged with you and our high priest for breakthrough salvation in the nations!

Kingdom Principle

Prayer is the key for opening the heavens and creating portals for GOD encounters in our region.

"Now when all people were baptized, it came to pass, that Jesus also being baptized, and praying, the heaven was opened."   Luke 3:21 KJV

A phenomenal event took place during our Lord's baptism. Heaven opened and GOD began to speak, three distinct things, which helped the Lord excel in His assignment. GOD declares "Thou art my beloved Son in thee I am well pleased "(Luke 3:22) *"Thou Art"*—God declared who Jesus was and gave Him *identity*. *"Beloved Son"*—God publicly *affirmed* Jesus in the eyes of the people. *"In whom I am well pleased"*—God gave Jesus the needed security of His acceptance and *approval*. The point of reference here is Christ was actually praying and a portal was opened to publicly release God's approval of His ministry. This fortified His assignment in establishing victorious living for all believers.

Many today have the charge to manifest phenomenal works for the furtherance of the Kingdom. However, open heavens and open portals are essential for us as it was for Christ and His earthly assignment.

As it was with our Lord, I decree so shall it be unto you. Open heavens, open portals and an immersing into your new assignment as you pray. May the voice of GOD bring identity, affirmation and security to you in your mandate as you pursue your purpose in Jesus Name!

Kingdom Principle

Prayer helps to bring believers into alignment with the Kingdom of GOD.

"And he said unto them, 'When ye pray, say, Our Father which art in Heaven, Hallowed be thy name. Thy Kingdom come. Thy will be done, as in Heaven, so in the Earth."

Luke 11:2 KJV

Prayer is one of the most viable threats against the destructive forces of darkness at work in the earth today. Satan fears, with untold dread, those who have a life of prayer and especially local churches that practice corporate prayer consistently. These kinds of believers will be found expanding without compromise. They understand the price to be paid in the kingdom of men, yet they will display an uncanny willingness to pay the price at any cost. GOD's grace will be evident in a mega way and their triumphs will be twice as great as their trials. I'm sure you too have had set backs and challenges that have overwhelmed you. For some of us these setbacks and challenges have shocked us to the core of our souls. However God designed us to withstand anything that hell would every release against us. This truth coupled with a life immersed in prayer proves to be a line of distinction in the spirit realm which yields to heaven breaking into the earth.

The Lord gave His disciples a clear blueprint on how they could get heaven to manifest in the earth, and that is to pray!! As we contend in prayer for His Kingdom to come in this generation our expectancy will come to another level and supernatural activity will increase in our midst. This will yield tremendous resources, consistency in breakthrough, an abundance of souls coming to the Kingdom and an elevation of desire for the Word of God in the nations.

May the fruit of stability in prayer among the members of our local church be established. May victory over the powers of darkness both personally and corporately come forth speedily, in Jesus name.

Kingdom Principle

7

Continuity in prayer qualifies the believer for divine appointment.

"These all continued with one accord in Prayer and Supplication with the women, and Mary the mother of Jesus, and with his brethren." Acts 1:14 KJV

"And when the day of Pentecost was fully come, they were all with one accord in one place." Acts 2:1 KJV

Continuity in prayer serves as a precursor in order to get the realities of heaven established in the earth. One of the realities is the promise of the coming of the Holy Spirit which the Lord declared prior to His ascension.

A group of 120 believers were laboring in prayer for 10 consecutive days. Then suddenly the promise of God breaks into the earth with the sound of a mighty rushing wind and cloven tongues of fire. Their steadfastness, consistency and discipline in prayer proved to be the catalyst for the fulfillment of the promise of God given by the Lord.

I believe the Lord desires to release more of Himself to this generation. Are you willing to gather with like minded believers and pray consistently until spiritual elevation, expansion, and increased capacity for your life, church and city occurs?

This will become relevant and tangible in the life of intercessors and ministries who are driven to see divine appointment fulfilled in their sphere of influence.

Kingdom Principle

Prayer during times of persecution releases the power of GOD to judge systems, institutions and kingdoms that hold believers captive.

"And at midnight Paul and Silas prayed, and sang praises unto GOD: and the prisoners heard them. And suddenly there was a great earthquake, so that the foundations of the prison were shaken: and immediately all the doors were opened, and every one's bands were loosed."

Acts 16:25-26 KJV

After the Apostle Paul cast the spirit of divination out of the young damsel her masters brought charges against them, the multitudes stir opposition against them, stripped them of their clothing, beat them and put them in jail. We are beginning to see common threads of this kind of hostility increasing in the nations through systems, institutions and kingdoms that are anti God.

Paul and Silas were destined to be destroyed if GOD had not intervened. Their discipline in ministering to the Lord and prayer proved to be vital in their release from captivity. An earthquake destroyed the foundation of the prison and every man's bands were loosed.

A praise and prayer meeting during a strategic time of the night opened the way for GOD's judgment to hit Phillipi and shake that territory. We too can share in the same results, if we choose to partner with GOD for greater works, and utilize prayer as the foundation for judging territorial powers.

There are many individuals and congregations alike who are in similar predicaments. The spirit of divination is trying to squeeze and choke the will of God out of them and literally crush their ministry. This is especially true for apostolic and prophetic ministries because of the spiritual levels they operate in.

The corporate gathering of apostolic and prophetic ministries are known to impact the spirit realm, thereby warranting spiritual attacks through systems, institutions and kingdoms in their territory. This is not to discredit other ministries who are not apostolic and prophetic but only to qualify the statement being made.

Therefore Satan's priority is to silence believers who have made destroying his kingdom their priority.

I speak strength over you to contend in prayer against spirits of divination. I command every assignment to silence, minimize your influence and limit your visibility to be broken in Jesus name.

Kingdom Principle

Prayer releases Kingdom keys of wisdom and revelation.

"That the GOD of our Lord Jesus Christ, the Father of glory, may give unto you the spirit of Wisdom and Revelation in the knowledge of him: The eyes of your understanding being enlightened; that ye may know what is the hope of his calling, and what the riches of the glory of his inheritance in the saints." Ephesians 1:17-18 KJV

One of the ways we can come into greater understanding of Christ and His mission is to pray. The Lord says in Jeremiah 33:3, *"Call unto me, and I will answer thee, and show thee great and mighty things, which thou knowest not"* Nothing should ever take the place of us studying GODs word, however, I don't believe that studying and not praying will serve the greater purposes of GOD. The combination of study and prayer helps to develop the believer and balance them out. All word and no spirit as well as, all spirit and no word are equally dangerous.

I received something very beneficial from the late Kenneth Hagin on praying Ephesians 1:17-18. He shared that before he reads or studies the Word he'd pray and ask GOD for wisdom and revelation from the word. I adopted this and for many years have enjoyed the blessing of walking in revelation of the Word. You too can enjoy open heavens and revelation for your life, assignment, ministry, education, business, family, etc if you'll simply ask GOD in prayer for the spirit of wisdom and revelation.

Bezaleel was an individual during the ministry of Moses who can be qualified as having the spirit of wisdom. He understood because of wisdom how to construct the tabernacle of Moses and make a reality of what was in the mind of Moses and God. (See Exodus 35:30-35)

Benefits of Wisdom:

Wisdom builds her house (Proverbs 24:3)
With Wisdom there is might (Daniel 2:20)

According to Ephesians 1:17 revelation is a spirit, which is defined as something revealed or disclosed, especially something not before realized. The Apostle Paul's prayer for the believers in Ephesus could be said this way "father I pray for you to reveal things that they have never realized before". I believe God wants to reveal things that have been hidden from us in order to advance His Kingdom. So as you pray for revelation expect God to show you things you've not seen before concerning His Kingdom.

Kingdom Principle

Prayer connects us to the grace of GOD in order to champion over life's issues.

"Likewise, ye husbands, dwell with them according to knowledge, giving honour unto the wife, as unto the weaker vessel, and as being heirs together of the Grace of Life; that your prayers be not hindered."   1 Peter 3:7 KJV

The ability to operate in elevated levels of unity is critical for kingdom advancement among believers. This is especially true, but not limited to, those who are married. Satan is aware of this verse, trust me on this one. The absence of unity and togetherness among covenant people is an invitation for the powers of darkness to access your life. Now some may say, "What does this have to do with prayer?" Well, notice how Peter says our prayers will be hindered and we will miss out on something that's especially vital for Kingdom living and that's **GRACE**.

Grace is defined as favour, kindness, loveliness, goodness and graciousness; joy, a kindness granted or desired, a benefit, benevolence honour or advantage. This meaning really highlights what we run the risk of losing or missing out on if the unity part is missing, which results in hindrances to our prayers being answered.

As an heir of grace for life you can maximize your time on the planet as you pray and enjoy the benefits of covenant relationships.

May you move forward in advancement of GOD's agenda, plan, and destiny for your life, and enjoy all of His goodness for you and champion over life's issues.

Kingdom Principle

Travailing in prayer helps develop and mature the believers in Christ.

"My little children, of whom I travail in birth again until Christ, be formed in you."   Galatians 4:19 KJV

The Galatians were under intense attack for their faith in Christ. The Apostle Paul humbled himself and began to travail in prayer so Christ would be formed in them.

Travail: to produce as a seed from (a mother, a plant, the earth), to bring forth or deliver through painful or excessive labor.

Form: to fashion, figuratively the nature.

Travailing in prayer until we see tangible fruit in our gatherings is a non-negotiable. Ministry, as we know it, is changing and those who refuse to embrace change will swiftly find their works obsolete and irrelevant in helping to birth and shape a generation for Christ. What we're laboring for is not another large gathering to boast in our ability to draw large crowds, but rather to see the nature of our King established in His people and righteous representation of Him in our spheres.

Christ labored while He physically walked the planet with the intent to bring many sons to glory; He's still laboring in eternity through intercession saving and impacting generations, though He's entered into rest. The mandate to intercede day and night, labor in the Word and stay in faith requires a strong work ethic.

The body of Christ is desperately in need of ministry gifts that can tune into the heart of GOD and embrace what He's releasing in order to develop and mature His people. This will cost you much, but the rewards will be even greater as the people of GOD are set free. God desires to have sons and daughters who can handle the affairs of His Kingdom.

As you travail and labor for Christ to be formed in you and those you're called to serve may you be found unmovable until an abundance of fruit is evident.

Kingdom Principle

12

Prayer affords us to secure a quiet and peaceable life in all godliness.

"I exhort therefore, that, first of all, Supplications, Prayers, Intercessions, and Giving Thanks, be made for all men. For kings and for all that are in authority; that we may lead a quiet and peaceable life in all godliness and honesty. For this is good and acceptable in the sight of GOD our savior."   I Timothy 2:1-3 KJV

"The first thing I want you to do is pray. Pray every way you know how, for everyone you know. Pray especially for rulers and their governments to rule well so we can be quietly about our business of living simply, in humble contemplation. This is the way our Savior GOD wants us to live."   I Timothy 2:1-3 MSG

We live in a time where global events, regardless of the time of day, can be instantly uploaded and go viral thanks to the wonderful world of social networking. Reports of the affairs of men can be revealed in a moment's notice.

This new found access to global events can also serve as a tremendous tool for the Church to pray for all men. I'm using the term "all men" generically for all people and the earthly governments they are joined to because of their nationality. The first thing we're admonished to do is pray. I like the way the Message translation brings out that we should pray every way we know how, for everyone, this is the way our Savior GOD wants us to live.

As gossip, slander, accusation and misleading information floods the multiple-channels of communication we have at our disposal today, we must embrace a life of prayer fueled with passion for all men.

With so much activity taking place in the nations and the civil unrest that's threatening even the stability of major powers, the saints are needed now in this moment of time like we've never been needed before. Taking the position to build houses of prayer for all people is no longer an option, but a must. As we pursue this mandate we can live on the fruit of a quiet and peaceable life in all godliness and honesty.

Kingdom Principle

Prayer provides liberty for the Word of GOD to flow freely and be glorified.

*"Finally brethren, pray for us, that the **Word** of the Lord may have free course, and be glorified even as it is with you: And that we may be delivered from unreasonable and wicked men: for all men have not faith."*

II Thessalonians 3:1-2 KJV

"One more thing, friends: Pray for us. Pray that the Master's Word will simply take off and race through the country to a groundswell of response, just as it did among you. And pray that we'll be rescued from these scoundrels who are trying to do us in. I'm finding that not all "believers" are believers. But the Master never lets us down. He'll stick by you and protect you from evil."

II Thessalonians 3:1-2 The Message

"For the rest, brethren, pray for us, that the word of the Lord may run and be glorified, even as also with you; and that we may be delivered from bad and evil men, for faith [is] not [the portion] of all. But the Lord is faithful, who shall establish you and keep [you] from evil."

II Thessalonians 3:1-2 The Darby

Prayer is one of the determining factors concerning the level of impact the Word of GOD will have. Apart from intercession the Word of God could potentially have minimal impact when preached in certain places, especially those places where it's never been proclaimed. The Apostle Paul understood this and asked the believers of Thessalonica to pray for him. Notice his prayer specifically requested for the word of the Lord to have free course and be glorified.

The Message translation says, "*Pray that the Master's Word will simply take off and race through the country to a groundswell of response...*" A groundswell speaks of a surge of support, approval or enthusiasm especially among the general public. Therefore apart from prayer the type of response we're looking for when the Gospel is preached could potentially be minimal.

The Darby translation says, "*Pray for us that the word of the Lord may run and be glorified...*"

Benefits of the Glory of GOD

The Glory of GOD is a shield - Psalm 3:2-3
The Glory of GOD Releases Dominion - Psalm 8:4-6
The Glory of GOD Is Essence of Life - Psalm 21:1-5
The Glory of GOD Is Our Refuge - Psalm 62:7
The Glory of GOD Is His Burning Presence - Zechariah 2:5
     and Psalm 105:39
The Glory of GOD Destroys Wickedness - II Thessalonians 1:7-9

The Glory of GOD Defends - Isaiah 4:4-5
The Glory of GOD Delivers - Psalm 79:9
The Glory of GOD Causes Good Things to Come Forth
Psalm 84:11

Satan hates the glory of GOD because it encompasses the weighty presence of GOD among His people. Prayer is a viable catalyst for the glory of GOD. The more liberty for ministry gifts to proclaim the word of GOD, the greater our experience will be in the glory. The church stands to gain so much more as the glory of GOD increases.

The King James translation says *"And that we may be delivered from unreasonable and wicked men: for all men have not faith."* There are demonic powers that inspire godless men to launch verbal and even physical attacks against ministry gifts that have high impact in the spirit realm. The Word is the precursor for the glory. Prayer for the safety and protection of these ministry gifts is important. For those called to nations hostile to the gospel of Christ, these verses carry a totally different meaning. Kingdom advancement is often met with resistance, but the prayers of the righteous prevail.

Kingdom Principle

Prayer empowers the believer to breakthrough obstacles and limitations.

"Likewise the Spirit also helpeth our infirmities: for we know not what we should pray for as we ought, but the Spirit Himself maketh intercession for us with groaning which can not be uttered. And he that searcheth the hearts knoweth what is the mind of the Spirit, because he maketh intercession for the saints according to the will of GOD. And we know that all things work together for good to them that love GOD, to them who are the called according to his purpose." Romans 8:26-28 KJV

There are times when all believers are confronted with life's circumstances and the lack of natural wisdom and insight on what to pray. You can know every scripture in the bible and still be confronted with not knowing what to pray that accurately addresses your situation.

However, our relationship with the Holy Spirit affords us an edge in this life where we can live from His burning presence in us. He teaches us, He comforts us, He guides or leads us, He warns us and He shows us things to come just to name a few of His assignments.

Yet Romans 8:26-28 reveals another assignment which is He will pray through us. Yes, the Holy Spirit prays perfect prayers through those who will yield their voices to Him.

There are spiritual things we need from GOD and there are spiritual things sent by Satan we need to breakthrough and overcome. Praying in tongues helps to build the spirit man inside of us. The more we pray in tongues the more readily we can respond to spiritual things. Human weaknesses that would seek to forbid us from advancing into next level agenda's ordained by GOD can also be overcome. The more we pray in tongues the more accurate and sensitive we become in spiritual matters.

Jude 1:20 says that as we pray in the Holy Ghost we build ourselves up on our most holy faith. We know without faith it's impossible to please GOD. So praying in tongues is yet another way of developing an intense walk of faith to perform exploits that will advance the Kingdom of our GOD. For further insight on this subject, I recommend our book, *"The Benefits of Praying In Tongues"*.

Kingdom Principle

15

Prayer fortifies the believer to mentally and physically to endure suffering.

"And he came out, and went, as he wont, to the Mount of Olives; and his disciples also followed him. And when he was at the place, he said unto them, pray that ye enter not into temptation. And he was withdrawn from them about a stone's cast, and kneeled down, and prayed, saying Father, if thou be willing, remove this cup from me: nevertheless not my will, but thine, be done. And there appeared an angel unto him from heaven, strengthening him. And being in agony he prayed more earnestly: and his sweat was as it were great drops of blood falling down to the ground. And when he rose up from prayer, and was come to his disciples, he found them sleeping for sorrow, And he said unto them, why sleep ye? Rise and pray, lest ye enter into temptation."

Luke 22:39-46 KJV

This passage of scripture highlights an event, which I deem as pivotal to Christ embracing his destiny, crucifixion by way of a cross. There's a very important principle revealed here concerning intercession which I believe is vital for every Christian who will live with holy abandonment. The Lord was engaged in tremendous warfare, humanity was weighing in the balances and the final hours for the very purpose for which He was born had now arrived in the realm of time. There was a horrible death He had to die. Intense scrutiny and mockery for a prolonged period of time was about to make its debut in the Lord's life. How would He handle it? How would He endure?

The answer is found in the place of prayer. The scripture records that He asked the disciples to pray that they enter not into temptation, which by implication means adversity. They were challenged by the Lord to pray not to enter into adversity, which often produces internal struggles when sacrifice in order to obey is required. The disciples failed miserably during one of the most grueling times of the Lord's life prior to the cross; when He needed them the most they were fast asleep.

The burdens and pressures that come with fulfilling divine assignments which have godly ramifications on generations to come aren't without a price. With so much at stake the Lord, engages in agonizing prayer until He's perspiring and passing blood through His sweat glands.

He is recorded in Matthew's gospel, as praying on three separate occasions after beckoning the disciples for help. This truth establishes the fact that even our Lord had to persevere in prayer until His mind, will, emotions and all that was in Him came into compliance.

There will be times when our confessions of certain scriptures, having others touch and agree or having hands laid on us simply won't provide the grace necessary to breakthrough. The requirement is that we agonize in prayer until GOD breaks in and strengthens us.

May grace be supplied unto you to rise in this season of your life and ministry. May you move in new levels of prayer that manifest rippling effects in the generations to come. May the goodness of GOD be your portion because you are paying the price now!

Kingdom Principle

Prayer that's done in secret produces open rewards.

16

5) And when thou prayest, thou shalt not be as the hypocrites are: for they love to pray standing in the synagogues and in the corners of the streets, that they may be seen of men. Verily I say unto you, They have their reward. 6) But thou, when thou prayest, enter into thy closet, and when thou hast shut thy door, pray to thy Father which is in secret; and thy Father which seeth in secret shall reward thee openly. 7) But when ye pray, use not vain repetitions, as the heathen do: for they think that they shall be heard for their much speaking. 8) Be not ye therefore like unto them: for your Father knoweth what things ye have need of, before ye ask him.

Matthew 6:5-8 (KJV)

5) "And when you come before God, don't turn that into a theatrical production either. All these people making a regular show out of their prayers, hoping for stardom! Do you think God sits in a box seat?] 6) "Here's what I want you to do: Find a quiet, secluded place so you won't be tempted to role-play before God. Just be there as simply and honestly as you can manage. The focus will shift from you to God, and you will begin to sense his grace. 7) "The world is full of so-called prayer warriors who are prayer-ignorant. They're full of formulas and programs and advice, peddling techniques for getting what you want from God. Don't fall for that nonsense. 8) This is your Father you are dealing with, and he knows better than you what you need.

Matthew 6:5-8 (MSG)

The Lord admonishes us on how we should pray in order get desired results. He also admonishes on how we're not to pray. He knows the things we have need of and if we desire rewards from the relationship we must embrace the order that He's established.

The first thing He challenges us to do is not draw attention to ourselves when praying. The Message Translation for Matthew 6:5 says *"and when you come before God don't turn that into a theatrical production..."* Sometimes prayer when not spirit inspired can be so scripted and godless that it appears to be for show. God is not interested in theatrics but rather empowering His people.

The need for a specific location is of grave importance. For instance a certain location in your house, car, or the local church itself could all be qualified as a specified location, in others words your prayer closet

It's in these specified places God sees us and visits us. The more consistent we are in praying from those locations the more presence we will have.

It's from this type of prayer activity that God begins to reward openly. Remember He knows the things we have need of according to Matthew 6:8.

May your prayers be inspired by God's Word and your commitment to advance His Kingdom. May a secret place be discovered by you and filled with the presence of God as you practice consistency in meeting Him. May open rewards bring volumes of breakthrough concerning you in Christ.

Kingdom Principle

17

Prayer fuels believers with boldness during times of crisis.

"And when they had prayed, the place was shaken where they were assembled together; and they were all filled with the Holy Ghost, and they spake the word of GOD with boldness."   Acts 4:31 KJV

Foundations are necessary for any building assignment whether it's a tangible or non-tangible project. Foundations serve as support systems on which physical structures and spiritual entities are established. For instance, the Church, a gathering of people physical but spiritual in nature has a foundation. The Lord declares that upon this rock He'd build His Church and the gates of hell would not prevail against it (Matthew 16:18).

There are structures both visible and invisible which have been built to serve the purposes of Satan. Their sole agenda is to provide consistent resistance against the Church by laws, regulations, media campaigns, etc or spiritual entities that are under the direct command of Satan.

After enduring a time of threatening from the council, the apostles were released and back to ministering the word. The miracle of the lame man getting healed activated great faith among the people and GOD was glorified. There was still a tension in the atmosphere and the apostles didn't take it lightly. They began praying and invoking the power of GOD over the territory. They prayed for GOD to give them boldness to speak His words and proclaim His message. They emphasized GOD stretching forth His hand releasing healing and great signs and wonders to be performed by the Name of Jesus.

Energized and intensified preaching that activates the miraculous during times of persecution is the result of intercession destined to activate the power of GOD. The apostle understood that the foundation supporting the territorial belief system, if they were to release the captives, required heightened supernatural activity.

Their pursuit of GOD resulted in a literal earthquake manifesting and multitudes being filled with the Holy Ghost. I decree the return of these days to the Church, our territories and nations.

Kingdom Principle

Prayer is influential in the plan of GOD concerning the days of man.

"In those days was Hezekiah sick unto death. And Isaiah the prophet the son of Amoz came unto him, and said unto him, Thus saith the Lord, Set thine house in order: for thou shalt die, and not live. Then Hezekiah turned his face toward the wall, and prayed unto the Lord, and said remember now, O Lord, I beseech thee, how I have walked before thee in truth and with a perfect heart and have done that which is good in thy sight. And Hezekiah wept sore. Then came the word of the Lord to Isaiah, saying, Go and say to Hezekiah, Thus saith the Lord, the GOD of David thy Father, I have heard thy prayer, I have seen thy tears: behold I will add unto thy days fifteen years."

Isaiah 38:1-5 KJV

GOD placed King Hezekiah under a death sentence. He was informed by the word of the Lord to set his house in order because death was his portion. The severity of this word would cause Christians today to break down and collapse.

However, this wasn't the case for King Hezekiah. His pursuit of life in prayer activated the power of GOD on his behalf. The prophet Isaiah was charged to revisit him, however this time with the word of life. We don't have to die before our time.

Intercession will increase our life span and prolong our days. Refuse to yield to any sickness or disease or judgment that has been on your life. Remember we can pray until God changes His mind about us. Invoke your covenant right to the healing power of GOD. Life and that more abundantly belongs to you. Turn to the wall as King Hezekiah did and pray until desired results come forth.

Kingdom Principle

19

Prayer creates access for divine intervention

"And it came to pass, when King Hezekiah heard it, that he rent his clothes, and covered himself with sackcloth, and went into the house of the Lord. And he sent Eliakim, which was over the household, and Shebna the scribe, and the elders of the priests, covered with sackcloth, to Isaiah the prophet the son of Amoz. And they said unto him, Thus saith Hezekiah, this day is a day of trouble, and of rebuke, and blasphemy: for the children are come to the birth, and there is not strength to bring forth."

II Kings 19:1-3 KJV

Situations, events and circumstances that have changed the course of history throughout the life of humanity are nothing new. However, we as saints have a say so in what happens in any given period of time. Our impact can become most potent and lasting when we take time to intercede and call upon GOD. Accurate articulation is critical to breaking through.

King Hezekiah understood the times in which he lived. He acknowledged a time of trouble, blasphemy and rebuke. Properly identifying resistance and hurdles to advancement will prove pivotal, especially in times of transition and expansion.

King Hezekiah synchs his prayer frequency with prophetic utterances by Isaiah and ultimately broke through. There are times when prophetic words can provide wisdom on how to develop prayer strategies so we can stay on target with proclaiming the heart of GOD.

The Lord intervened and wrought a great deliverance for Israel because of prayer. The Assyrians were minimized by GOD, their leader defeated by his own sons and a mighty angel sent by GOD demolished the world's most powerful army during that time of history.

Let us purpose to make and shape history as we stand in the place of prayer and secure the birthing of promises ordained by GOD for our generation.

Kingdom Principle

20

Prayer will provide restoration for displaced leaders.

"Now therefore restore the man his wife; for he is a prophet, and he shall pray for thee, and thou shalt live: and if thou restore her not, know thou that thou shalt surely die, thou, and all that are thine."

Genesis 20:7 KJV

"So Abraham prayed unto GOD: and GOD healed Abimelech and his wife and his maidservants and they bare children."

Genesis 20: 17 KJV

Abraham a prophet of GOD found himself in a very challenging situation where he lies and causes Sarah, his wife to fall into the hands of King Abimelech. Sarah was a vital part of the purposes of heaven during her day, yet she was put in a position that could potentially abort the plan of GOD. Many of us at one junction or another have compromised because we were unaware of the destiny ordained for us by GOD. As a result, we engaged in activity, got involved with people or camped out in places contrary to the plans of GOD. This was the case with Abraham and Sarah. GOD was not about to allow this to happen so He invades the dream realm of

King Abimelech and seizes his life, bringing it to a complete halt.

Abraham, in verse 7, had to pray for King Abimelech to be released from the retribution GOD had allowed to come on his household.

The word, *"pray"* in the referenced passage comes from the Hebrew word palal (paw-lal) key 6419 which means to judge, to intercede, pray, entreat, to make supplication; this definition normally defines the kind of prayer rendered when we pray for people who are in distress or challenging situations. Our aim is to get GOD in the situation in order for a reversal of the current condition to take place.

Abraham prays and according to Genesis 20:17, GOD heals Abimelech, his wife, his maidservants and removes barrenness from them.

There are many that stand in need of the type of intercession prayed by Abraham on behalf of King Abimelech. As you continue in Kingdom prayer, may kings be loosed from their failures and families restored from evil plans as you advocate for justice.

Kingdom Principle

21

Prayer gives us direct access to angelic powers stationed in our regions.

"Yea whiles I was speaking in prayer, even the man Gabriel, whom I had seen in the vision at the beginning, being caused to fly swiftly, touched me about the time of evening oblation. And he informed me, and talked with me, and said, O Daniel, I am now come forth to give thee skill and understanding."

Daniel 9:21-22 KJV

Understanding the role of angels and the angelic realm is critical for the current season of the Church. The mandates we have to impact nations through political, social, educational and economical sphere's requires we forge a divine partnership with our invisible arsenal of warriors and messengers

Angels are identified in the scripture as: Ministering Spirits (Hebrews 1:14), as Watchers (Daniel 4:17), as Seraphim's (Isaiah 6:2), as Cherubim's (Isaiah 37:16). They are available for us and ordained by GOD to serve with us in the advancement of the Kingdom of GOD. They assist us in warfare, they provide protection, they prepare pathways, they provide supernatural insight and they fight against our enemies.

The prophet Daniel was immersed deep within Babylon and was found contending for insight concerning the plight of his people Israel. While fasting, confessing the sins of his people, repenting, praying and making supplications before GOD, a powerful angelic being burst into the visible realm. He engages Daniel and informs him that his coming was strictly for the purpose of imparting skill to understand. Supernatural insight was granted to Daniel because of his relentless pursuit of GOD to know the destiny of his people.

There is an advanced level of knowledge and insight coming to the intercessors of this generation who will dare contend for the wisdom of the Ancient of Days. Along with the work of the Holy Spirit, there's coming a climatic shifting to the saints in every nation regardless of our current positioning. Angels are being activated to breakthrough invisible barriers and reveal the eternal purposes of GOD for us. Keep contending for understanding and receive the assistance of those ministering spirits that are sent forth to us, the heirs of salvation. For more insight on the role of angels, refer to our book *Ministering Spirits, Engaging the Angelic Realm.*

Kingdom Principle

22

Prayer will help form angelic partnerships in ministry assignment.

"Then said he unto me, fear not Daniel: for from the first day that thou didst set thine heart to understand and chasten thyself before thy GOD, thy words were heard and I am now come for thy words. But the prince of the kingdom of Persia withstood me one and twenty days: but lo, Michael, one of the chief princes, came to help me; and remained there with the kings of Persia."

Daniel 10:12-13 KJV

There are times when we desperately need answers from GOD, yet there's no response. To the novice and the anxious this may present very indifferent case scenarios. However, the prophet Daniel chose another course of action which I believe is vital for intercessors today who are assigned to churches, regions and territories that desperately need to hear from GOD. Daniel prayed consistently.

The streaming of spirit inspired words, along with declaring the inspired Word (scriptures) in prayer will prove to be a formidable weapon when challenged with delay. Psalm 103:20 declares, *"Bless the Lord ye, His angels that excel in strength, that do His commandments, hearkening unto the voice of His word."* Angels, the heavenly host and the powers of darkness respond to the Word. The more we pray the word and emphasize it while praying, the greater assistance we will have from those who excel in strength in our respective sphere's and realms of influence. One thing Satan can't handle is a disciplined saint who will obey, despite the opposition raging against them.

A chief prince in rank from the angelic realms comes to Daniel's aide because of his consistency in prayer. The messenger that Daniel encountered in chapter 9 returns this time for Daniel's words. The emphasis here is the "words" of Daniel. The satanic resistance in the invisible realm above the physical territory from which Daniel was praying was being guarded by the prince of Persia. This was obviously a principality of which the Apostle Paul tells us in *Ephesians 6:12 "for we wrestle not against flesh and blood, but against principalities..."* which can be simply defined as a realm or territory governed by a prince. GOD also has princes that He desires to govern in realms and territories where the saints are present as we maintain consistency in prayer.

Angelic hosts assigned to you come forth to assist you in divine partnership for your region.

Kingdom Principle

23

Prayer grants access to the new things of God.

"That thou mightest know the certainty of those things, wherein thou hast been instructed. THERE was in the days of Herod, the king of Judea, a certain priest named Zacharias, of the course of Abia: and his wife was of the daughters of Aaron, and her name was Elisabeth. And they were both righteous before GOD, walking in all commandments and ordinances of the Lord blameless. And they had no child, because that Elisabeth was barren, and they both were now well stricken in years. And it came to pass, that while he executed the priest's office before GOD in the order of his course, According to the custom of the priest's office, his lot was to burn incense when he went into the temple of the Lord. And when the whole multitude of the people were praying without at the time of incense. And there appeared unto him an angel of the Lord standing on the right side of the altar of incense."   Luke 1:4-11 KJV

The very essence of a new move being birthed in the earth is captured in the referenced passages. Human activity was elevated and people were now being aligned to further the plans of GOD during this time of history that has changed the lives of multitudes in every generation since that time.

GOD was preparing the way for Christ, the Son of GOD, to come forth. Zacharias was executing a model of ministry that was about to be radically transformed. Something prophetic was coming that was initiating a "suddenly of GOD" moment. The key to this activity was being generated through the multitudes that were praying.

Zacharias was burning incense on the altar which is symbolic of prayer. Suddenly an angel of the Lord appears by the altar and begins to inform Zacharias about a miracle conception that was going to happen from his union with Elizabeth. Zacharias wasn't compliant so GOD shut his mouth for a season.

John the Baptist was born out of this encounter and became the voice that prepared the way for the coming of the Lord. As multitudes gather, to pray and build altars, may forerunners of our day be birth to prepare people for Christ our King.

Kingdom Principle

24

Prayer breaks the strongholds of generational and corporate captivity.

"And it came to pass in process of time, that the king of Egypt died: and the children of Israel sighed by reason of the bondage, and they cried, and their cry came up unto GOD by reason of the bondage. And GOD heard their groaning, and GOD remembered his covenant with Abraham, with Isaac, and with Jacob. And GOD looked upon the children of Israel, and GOD had respect unto them." Exodus 2:23-25 KJV

The cries which were ascending from the mud pits of Egypt would prove lethal to the strongholds entrenched in the spirit realm. GOD had made a promise over 400 years prior to this cry being released to Abram. He promised that after 400 years of captivity that He'd bring His people out of bondage with great substance. (See Genesis 15:6-17)

The word, "cry" used in Exodus 2:23 is the Hebrew word Shav'ah which simply means *"a cry for help"*. Because of the loving and merciful nature of GOD, HE cannot remain neutral or inactive when HIS people ask for HIS help. Like any father would when his children are in danger, GOD is sure to respond when HE hears us cry out to HIM in prayer.

It was this cry that caused GOD to raise up a deliverer which he sent into Egypt not only to bring about their deliverance from captivity, but also to release HIS supernatural blessings of favor, prosperity and protection to them.

*"And the children of Israel did according to the word of Moses; and they borrowed of the Egyptians jewels of silver and jewels of gold and raiment: And the LORD gave the people favour in the sight of the Egyptians, so much that they lent unto them such things as they required. And they spoiled the Egyptians." (*Exodus 11:35*)*

The time of exodus from captivity had come to the children of Israel, yet the Pharaoh of that day was non-compliant with the prophetic word that would ultimately render his demise. The power of GOD had now fallen in Egypt and a battle of epic proportion was on the horizon.

Exodus 3:7 and Exodus 6:5 emphasize the fact that GOD heard the cry and groans of His people and came down to address their oppressor. The covenantal agreement with Abram was at stake. GOD isn't a man that He should lie (Numbers 23:19). He was going to make good on His promise of deliverance and He did by manifesting ten plagues that literally broke the spirit of

Egypt. This miracle judgment was initiated by a corporate cry of covenant people.

"In that day there shall be an altar to the Lord in the midst of the land of Egypt and a pillar at the border thereof to the Lord. And it shall be for a sign and for a witness unto the Lord of host in the land of Egypt: for they shall cry unto the Lord because of the oppressors and he shall send them a savior and a great one and he shall deliver them." (Isaiah 19:19-20)

As our congregations gather to intercede, the anointing that will descend on us for the justice of GOD will usher in prophetic fulfillments. Multitudes will be set free from the powers of darkness. The strongmen of their captivity will stumble and perish at the presence of our GOD. Our prayers and intercession will lead to altars being established in the midst of our cities and pillars (garrisons) at our borders. This will be the witness of our GOD among us. Our cry, as in Exodus 2, will invoke GODs presence and great deliverance will be the result.

I declare that breakthrough of mega proportions have now descended on us and our cities.

Kingdom Principle

25

Prayer releases the spirit of grace and supplication.

"And I will pour upon the house of David, and upon the inhabitants of Jerusalem, the spirit of grace and of supplications: and they shall look upon me whom they have pierced, and they shall mourn for him, as one mourneth for his only son, and shall be in bitterness for him, as one that is in bitterness for his firstborn."

Zechariah 12:10 KJV

In every generation, with every movement of GOD, there is a need for the grace of GOD. The prophet Zechariah understands grace as a manifestation of the Spirit and precursor for supplications. Prayers of supplications are *earnest prayers where a superior one stoops or bends low to aide and assist an inferior.* This is why prayers of supplication must be energized with the spirit of grace.

It is because of GOD's grace that Christ was able to access the planet. Remember, by grace we are saved through faith. The plan of GOD to reconcile us was a work of grace. The King of glory stooped low to draw us out of bondage. This is a powerful truth that GOD desire's to play out over and over from generation to generation.

"And the child grew and waxed strong in the spirit filled with wisdom and the grace of GOD was upon him." (Luke 2:40)

"And Jesus increased in wisdom and stature and in favor with GOD and with Man." (Luke 2:52)

The Lord required grace to operate in the earth and fulfill His assignment to redeem man from his sins and restore us back to GOD. As mentioned before, grace also translates to favor. The favor Christ operated in also impacted the realm of men. As we move in our mandates to pray and intercede for the Kingdom of GOD to manifest, there will be the need for alliances with earthly institutions governed by men. The favor of GOD is the catalyst which opens the doors we need to advance.

The spirit of grace will energize our intercession with favor that will cause the kindness of GOD and man to be released unto us. This type of intercession is also necessary in order to get the masses to fix their eyes on Christ our King, who suffered for all. Grace to compel and accurately intercede for the harvest of this generation is available.

GOD is currently cultivating a new dependency of Him and many will rise in this day and age with new capacity in prayer; their supplication, prayer, giving of thanks and intercession is going to provide integral components in their place of service. The Lord has released a clarion call and divine summons for grace carriers to arise and embrace the Kingdom mandate of prayer.

My prayer is for you to be found faithful, turning the hearts and souls of many to Him by the grace that's in you.

Kingdom Principle

26

Prayer removes the lingering effects of loss and captivity.

"And the Lord turned the captivity of Job, when he prayed for his friends: also the Lord gave Job twice as much as he had before."   Job 42:10 KJV

"After Job had interceded for his friends, GOD restored his fortune-and then doubled it!   Job 42:10 MSG

When we position ourselves to pray and intercede for others with visible needs and challenges in our own lives GOD will deliver us, turn our captivity and set us free from bondage. This quality epitomizes an intrinsic value of character which we have access to in Christ. He suffered and endured an atrocious time of public humiliation and injustice. Yet, Christ refused to break the cycle of His suffering or negotiate His way out. As a result, GOD highly exalted Him and gave Him a name above every other name.

There are trials and times of suffering that serve as means for ascending to next level ministry and breakthrough in our assignments. A willingness to forgive and not internalize our trials, but embrace life and all it heralds at us as part of our Kingdom mandate.

Just as Job prayed for his friends who in actuality accused him of a wrong while he was already under the scrutiny of suffering and agonizing lose of his family, serves as a great example for us today on how to overcome personal lose and deliverance from captivity. Once this is grasped by the believer tremendous victories against the powers of darkness will become our reality. This is especially vital for intercessors and those who have prayer assignments in the local church.

May restoration, expansion and an abundance of things be ministered unto you as you pray the purposes of GOD for those you're called to serve.

Kingdom Principle

27

Prayer provides healing for lands and the citizens that dwell in them.

"If my people, which are called by my name, shall humble themselves, and pray, and seek my face, and turn from their wicked ways; then will I hear from heaven, and will forgive their sin, and will heal their land. Now mine eyes shall be open, and mine ears attent to the prayer that is made in this place."   II Chronicles 7:14-15 KJV

These two verses reveal a powerful truth concerning the prayers of the saints and the literal impact they have on the physical land which we occupy. This is also prophetic because we can't separate people from the land in which they live.

The capacity of the intercessor to call on GOD, practice humility, pray and seek the face of GOD and turn from their wicked ways will have direct impact on the land. GOD desires to hear and respond but the principles that govern righteous living must be adhered to. Many, however, have attempted to stand in territories ruled by demons and not deal with their own wickedness and eventually were consumed by what was controlling the land. Satan understands that the more participation he gets the more influence he has over people in any given territory.

We are confronted with multiple challenges which constantly seek to defile the lands which we occupy. Idolatry, human sacrifice whether through acts of violence or legalized procedures that allow blood to be shed, the land will become defiled. Notice how the sacrifice was rendered to devils which are connected to idols. The advancing of the Kingdom of GOD is highly associated with warfare. Intercessors who fail to apply knowledge concerning the activity of the land or physical territory they're planted in or sent to will find themselves in confrontations that seem impossible to win. We can win and prevail.

I decree that the eyes of the Church's understanding, is being enlightened and we are arising to properly deal with our lands, territories and regions in order for *Kingdom expansion* to come forth.

Kingdom Principle

28

Prayer helps to birth territorial promises.

"And Elijah said unto Ahab, Get thee up, eat and drink; for there is a sound of abundance of rain. So Ahab went up to eat and to drink. And Elijah went up to the top of Carmel; and cast himself down upon the Earth, and put his face between his knees. And said to his servant, Go up now, look toward the sea. And he went up and looked, and said, There is nothing. And he said, Go again seven times. And it came to pass at the seventh time, that he said, Behold, there ariseth a little cloud out of the sea, like a man's hand. And he said, Go up, say unto Ahab, Prepare thy chariot, and get thee down, that the rain stop thee not."

I Kings 18:41-44 KJV

It's our prayers that help synchronize the activity of earth with heaven. In Matthew 6:10, Jesus tells us to pray for GOD's kingdom and will on the earth to align with its manifestation in heaven. It is through the activity of prayer that we are enabled to pull GOD's heavenly initiatives out of the spiritual realm into the earth. The LORD declared to Peter, *"that whatsoever we bind on earth shall be bound in heaven and whatsoever we loose on earth shall be loosed in heaven..."* (Matthew

16:19). It is our prayer that activates the supernatural power of GOD to manifest in the earth.

Elijah put's these principles mentioned above to task. His charge is one which required heavens intervention. Israel under King Ahab's leadership is involved in occult activity through Baal worship. Elijah is sent to declare the verdict of the King of Glory to the nation. His words lock up the heavens; drought and famine establish a death grip on the nation for 3.5 years.

Elijah experiences the preserving power of GOD and all that come into contact with him are also blessed. Being properly positioned to hear the voice of GOD and take necessary actions is critical to our well being during times like that of Elijah. As nations are undergoing major overhauls and governments are experiencing revolts and civil discord we as saints must be able to hear clearly and take evasive actions in intercession.

Elijah ultimately gets the release from heaven to pray for the sanction to be lifted and it was through his deep commitment in prayer that the death grip was lifted off the nation of Israel. The scriptures don't give us a timeline as to how long it took, but Elijah's servant was charged 7 times to go check for rain. This implies to me that it was no easy task to get the rains released. Through labor and travail a cloud finally arises from the sea and the daunting task of getting the rain released was fulfilled. Those who are called to these realms of intercession possess tremendous stamina, resilience and grace.

May the Lord add to you all the necessities for the journey you're called to in Him.

Kingdom Principle

29

Prayer led by leadership helps the local church excel in their covenant assignments.

"And he stood before the altar of the Lord in the presence of all the congregation of Israel and spread forth his hands. For Solomon had made a brazen scaffold, of five cubits long, and five cubits broad, and three cubits high, and had set it in the midst of the court: and upon it he stood, and kneeled down upon his knees before all the congregation of Israel and spread forth his hands toward heaven. And said, O Lord GOD of Israel, there is no GOD like thee in the heaven, nor in the earth; which keepest covenant and shewest mercy unto thy servants that walk before thee with all their hearts:"

II Chronicles 6:12-14 KJV

King Solomon enjoyed the generational blessing that flowed from his father King David who was known for warring and worship, yet undeniably he was one of the most formidable intercessors in the Old Testament. King Solomon received the impartation and in this junction of his life the mantle of intercession was activated to intercede for the nation of Israel.

King Solomon is classified as one of the wisest in scripture, yet he understood the importance of keeping GOD involved in the many dimensions of leading covenant people. His pursuit of GOD on behalf of the nation of Israel corporately leading the charge in prayer is a model worthy of duplication today.

It's interesting to note that He stood before the altar, according to the referenced verse. The priests were the ones who were delegated the responsibility of ministering unto GOD before the altar; however, we see King Solomon standing before the altar with his hands spread forth. Solomon understood the charge of leading required divine insight, intervention and guidance.

The altar served as a means of contact with GOD through prayer. An altar also serves as a place of connection between heaven and earth. Solomon also understood that the well being of GOD'S covenant people would be a direct result of his leadership as their earthly king. Solomon wanted GOD in his realm or sphere, so he began to invoke His presence in prayer. I'm convinced when leaders assume this kind of responsibility, revival and unusual spiritual activity will begin to flood the nations at an accelerated rate.

King Solomon's quest to lead righteously serves as the foundation for his life of prayer as a leader.

He ultimately releases a series of prayers and begin to cry out for GOD's intervention for his citizens at home and abroad. No situation was off limits and King Solomon was bent on praying for GOD's hand to be upon his nation. He knew that trying times were inevitable, but also his experience in witnessing GOD's grace towards his father King David that the Lord was a GOD who would not forsake him especially during times of affliction. (See II Chronicles 6:19-42)

Kingdom Principle

30

Prayer serves as a type of power supply line.

"Confess to one another therefore your faults (your slips, your false steps, your offenses, your sins and pray also for one another, that you may be healed and restored to a spiritual tone of mind and heart. The earnest heartfelt, continued prayer of a righteous man makes tremendous power available dynamic in its working."

James 5:16 AMP

The Apostle James provides tremendous insight into the dynamics of a life inspired through intercession. The heart of any ministry gift will prove to be invaluable when all is said and done. I coined this phrase from a prophet who is a tremendous blessing to the body of Christ and I quote "The heart of an intercessor is their greatest weapon". This statement is in line with James 5:16 (amplified), where we are admonished to confess our faults, slips, etc to one another in order to be healed and restored to a spiritual tone of mind and heart. I'm convinced that one of the many reasons for watered down prayer is being on the wrong frequency as it relates to our spiritual tone and the condition of our heart. It's one thing to pray, but a whole new ball game to pray and have access to GOD's heart and breakthrough. The following list of hindrances to answered prayer is included in "*Pray without Ceasing: a Believer's Guide to Effective Intercession*":

1) Dishonor of Covenant Relationships
2) Sin & Carnality
3) Doubt & Unbelief
4) Fear
5) Double-Mindedness
6) Witchcraft & Iniquity
7) Unforgiveness
8) Pride
9) Lack of Perseverance
10) Wrong Motives
11) Spiritual Resistance
12) Unrighteousness

The Apostle James continues by declaring, "The earnest heartfelt prayers of a RIGHTEOUS man make tremendous power made available." The King James Version states, "the effectual fervent". The word, "*effectual*" comes from the Greek word (energo) which means "*to be active and efficient*". While "*fervent*" means "*to boil become hot like liquid, to glow*". So the intercessor, who has a life of prayer that's effectual and fervent, could be classified as one who prays and becomes so active until they are boiling with intense heat, literally glowing. This is such a powerful word picture revealing why we need to be intense when we pray. The result is tremendous power being made available.

Sometimes the regions and territories where we assemble lacks breakthrough, spiritual cleansing and awakening in part to limited intercession. In the mid 1990's my city, Chicago suffered a tremendous heat wave which ripped through the mid-west and hundred's died due to the sweltering inferno that blanketed the region. It was like the gateway of hell had opened in our city. The power supply company lacked the infrastructure to meet the needs of paying customers who put an overwhelming demand on power supply plants owned by the utility company. As a result roaming blackouts were implemented during peak daytime hours to ease the demand. This, of course, led to a major overhauling in the days to follow; yet, people were suffering and found the heat to be unbearable.

This is true in the spirit realm as well. There are times when the needs of people in a physical region become so demanding and the frailties of the Church are exposed. The Church Jesus is responsible for building, is one of which the gates of hell shall not prevail against, yet when darkness rules and boast itself as the power of a region we come under direct indictment. We are seeing this scenario play out all over the earth. This is especially true when murder, rape, corruption and false religions begin to rise in territories where there are present truth Churches. The lack of effectual fervent prayer is the major reason. There is dynamic (explosive) power made available when we raise the level on our prayer thermostat! What an awesome opportunity we have to extend the Kingdom through prayer.

It's my heartfelt prayer for believers all around the globe to come forth and take spiritual responsibility for the regions and nations we're called to, through effectual fervent prayer.

May the fires of prayer burn in you and a holy pursuit to contend in intercession until GOD breaks open the heavens over your region and comes down like a steady cleansing rain; redeeming, restoring, refreshing and reviving!

Kingdom Principle

31

Prayer is a momentum builder that will cause multitudes in the cities and nations to seek the Lord.

"And the inhabitants of one city shall go to another, saying, Let us go speedily to pray before the Lord, and to seek the Lord of hosts: I will go also. Yea, many people and strong nations shall come to seek the Lord of hosts in Jerusalem, and to pray before the Lord. Thus saith the Lord of hosts; In those days it shall come to pass, that ten men shall take hold out of all languages of the nations, even shall take hold of the skirt of him that is a Jew, saying, We will go with you: for we have heard that GOD is with you." Zechariah 8:21-23 KJV

The church is on the brink of her greatest hour of displaying the power of GOD! The identity of the church and the establishment of her voice in the heavens and the earth are contingent upon how she prays. The prophetic word of Zechariah could easily be looked upon as just a literal prophecy for literal Israel. If we limit the prophecies to literal Israel and exclude the church we run the risk of withdrawing ourselves from prophetic purposes ordained for us. The Lord, in Luke 24:31 opened the eyes of His disciples; in Luke 24:32 He opened the scriptures to them and in Luke 24:45 He opened their understanding that they might understand the scriptures. The spirit of revelation is essential to helping us understand what the will of the Lord is for us. Zechariah 8:20 reveals the gathering of people and the inhabitants from many different cities coming together to pray. GOD is raising up armies of intercessors and He's placing a supernatural attraction on us to gather multitudes from regions all around the globe. This is one of the visible signs we should be contending for if revival is our target.

Notice how verse 21 gives further insight into what's causing the multitudes to gather; the spirit of prayer is being stirred and released into the earth. The movement that sparked the multitudes to seek the Lord is what I call, *"The Global Prayer Movement".* Intercessory prayer is critical for harvesting the earth. There are many who will not come to know the goodness of GOD until someone in the earth begins to pave a pathway for them to come.

Then said He unto His disciples, *"The harvest truly is plenteous, but the laborers are few; PRAY ye therefore the Lord of the harvest, that he will send forth laborers into his harvest"* (Matthew 9:37-38). The key is connecting to the Lord of the harvest. Jesus is proclaiming to the earth His Lordship over the harvest; and the way we are to access the harvest is by crying out to Him in prayer.

The remaining verses show a progression from the people who make up cities and the impact they have on strong nations coming to seek the Lord. In verse 22 there is an increase of desire for GOD from cities to actual nations seeking Him. Jesus is the desire of the nations and the church must align herself with Christ if we are to see such an awesome display of His power to harvest the nations come to pass. The nations are coming to seek Him and to pray before Him. They are coming, looking for Him who is a JEW, Jesus Christ our King. We, as believers in Christ, are all Jews according to the inward circumcision of the heart, "*But he is a Jew, which is one inwardly; and circumcision is that of the heart, in the spirit, and not in letter; whose praise is not of men, but of GOD*" (Romans 2:29).

I decree the grace of GOD for intercession increases in your life; as you persevere and hasten the glorious coming of our Lord. Remember, its Christ in us the hope of glory.

Kingdom Principle

32

Prayer and fasting helps to execute redemptive works.

³⁶And there was one Anna, a prophetess, the daughter of Phanuel, of the tribe of Aser: she was of a great age, and had lived with an husband seven years from her virginity; ³⁷And she was a widow of about fourscore and four years, which departed not from the temple, but served God with fastings and prayers night and day. ³⁸And she coming in that instant gave thanks likewise unto the Lord, and spake of him to all them that looked for redemption in Jerusalem. Luke 2:36-38 KJV

The depth of Anna's prophetic assignment was not limited to her capacity to prophesy and declare, "thus says the Lord", but rather through her spirit inspired intercession. Prophets are of grave importance in the place of prayer. Their ability to see and hear helps the local church excel in prayer, releasing powerful streams of utterance that help the saints prevail in their call and destiny.

Her tenure of ministry was directly connected to the fulfillment of a promise made to a man name Simeon. Anna abided in the temple of GOD and established her placement. She knew the importance of prophetic positioning as she sensed, by the Spirit of the dawning, the most significant time in human history about to make its debut. She stood before GOD continually and refused to allow the noise of society to cause her to miss GOD.

Anna had tremendous capacity to encourage and deliver people. There are people joined to us who are depending on our effectiveness in prayer. The kind of prayer that preserves, keeps alive and energizes destinies.

The Lord is raising up Anna type companies of prophets who know their place of authority. They will be found in the house of GOD ushering in new movements of the Spirit, exhorting the saints concerning the hope of the Gospel and birthing "deliverers" who will bring refreshing and salvation to many. Are you an "Anna" type intercessor?

Do you have a desire for redemptions in your region? As a believer do you hunger for more than prophetic utterance? Are you concerned about the house of God? If so you could very well be an Anna type intercessor.

Kingdom Principle

33

Prayer keeps the fire burning on the altar.

"The fire on the altar must be kept burning and never allowed to go out. Every morning the priest shall put firewood on it, arrange the burnt offering on it, and burn the fat of the fellowship offering. The fire must always be kept burning on the altar and never allowed to go out.*"*
Leviticus 6:12-13 Good News Translation

"Whence, also he is able to save completely those who approach by him to GOD, always living to intercede for them."
Hebrews 7:25 Darby Translation

The Levitical priest had the responsibility to keep the fire burning on the altar. The fire was to burn continually and never allowed to go out. This is a prophetic picture of the way we're to conduct prayer in the local church as priest. Continually and without ceasing is the charge we have in communing with GOD and keeping the fire of His presence strong in our midst!

Jesus, our High Priest, forever lives to make intercession. This is vital for the church today because our intercession now provides a divine connection to the harvest of souls in our territories and nations.

The need for prayer alters:

Abraham builds an alter, offers a sacrifice and GOD is moved to establish covenant with him. This would lead ultimately to influence and impact people yet to be born. Remember that Abraham was a prophet that had a strong life of prayer. (Genesis 12:6-8, Genesis 15:7-18)

Isaac, Abraham's seed is in a territory gripped by famine. GOD's covenant promise with Abraham caused Isaac to prevail. He builds an alter calls upon God and provision was released in his life during a famine (See Genesis 26)

Jacob continues in the legacy of his fathers. He too builds alter and comes into the favor of GOD. (See Genesis 28 and 35)

In every generation, since the days of Noah, GOD has sought for those who would stand before Him, plug up the gaps in the walls of their nation and defend their land. As the prophets, priests and princes forsook the ways of GOD and opened Israel up for destruction through their greed, covetousness and idolatry, so have our leaders of this day. GOD's mercy is available for our land if we'll rise, build alter and stand before Him on behalf of our land.

Just as the priest of old were charged to minister before the alters unto GOD, today as priest alters are still significant for us. Remember the principle, the fire on the alter must never go out. I pray for an encounter today in your life with the GOD who answers by fire. May the altar of your heart be full of His consuming fire. Lord, let mantles for governmental prayer come on your people, even your priest.

Kingdom Principle

34

Prayer empowers believers to stand in times of adversity

"And take heed to yourselves, lest at anytime your hearts be overcharged with surfeiting, drunkenness and cares of this life, and so that day come upon you unawares. For as a snare shall it come on all them that dwell on the face of the whole Earth. Watch ye therefore, and pray always, that ye may be accounted worthy to escape all these things that shall come to pass, and to stand before the Son of man." Luke 21:34-35 KJV

Sobriety is paramount for any assignment we have in advancing the Kingdom of GOD. The heart of an intercessor is the greatest asset we have in serving our generation. We must take drastic measures in keeping it pure.

Luke provides three areas where we are to be watchful.

He charges us to guard our hearts from surfeiting, which literally means overindulgence or excess. Drunkenness and worldly cares are the other two areas which I feel directly influences a person's heart. I believe the cares of life will drive one to function from an intoxicated state, which may cause people to become aloof and unaware of the times and as a result they get snared or trapped.

We on the other hand as saints are admonished to watch and pray. This task would be almost impossible if we were entangled with any of the three things described by Luke that are in the earth. The Kingdom Mandate we have, also demands that we function from our position in Christ and be in the earth, yet not of the earth. In order to liberate the bound and set the captive free we need to function with high levels of diplomacy and embrace the immunity we have in the Kingdom of GOD.

I decree the adversity of the nations and generations will not serve as a tool to defeat you in your assignment. The King of Glory is in you and with you. As you intercede and pray for the destiny of those you're called to, be strengthened with might and may your eyes see the fruit of your labor as you advance the Kingdom of GOD.

Kingdom Principle

Prayer helps to destroy works of defilement and implements divine order in the "House of God"

And Jesus went into the temple of God, and cast out all them that sold and bought in the temple, and overthrew the tables of the moneychangers, and the seats of them that sold doves. And he said unto them, It is written, My house shall be called a house of prayer, but ye have made it a den of thieves. And the blind and the lame came to him in the temple, and he healed them.

Matthew 21:12-14

The entrance of the Lord into the temple of God during those days provides a clear picture of His position concerning the house of God. He begins to address the works of defilement by physically overthrowing tables and seats. A table represents a place of transaction, communion or fellowship while seats represent positions of judgment, God's throne, or a position of authority to name a few. The word "overthrow" means to turn upside down, that is to upset, literally to disturb. This word is important if we are to understand the Lord's passion for the house of God. He literally disturbed the order of temple activity connected to moneychangers and dove sellers. Moneychangers could easily represent covetousness, greed, and financial injustice in the house of God. The selling of doves could easily represent misplaced merchandising, misplaced value for the anointing.

After this demonstration of zeal the Lord declares "my house shall be call a house of prayer, but you have made it a den of thieves." The Lord was simply enforcing the prophecy of Isaiah 56:7. The key word being "house" which mean dwelling or family in both Hebrew and Greek. The significance of this is the fact that Jesus was a family or dwelling place of prayer which will serve as a means of establishing divine order. Once this revelation is fully birthed in the church we'll begin to see and witness with our own eyes the blind and lame supernaturally delivered. The blind could represent those who are literally blind but those who are spiritually blind; the lame could represent those who are literally crippled and those who are spiritually crippled. The fact is order in His gives way to the supernatural.

Kingdom Principle:

The daily needs of people mandates leader to give themselves to prayer and the ministry of the word.

But we will give ourselves continually to prayer and to the ministry of the word. Acts 6:4

The initial verses of Acts 6 highlights issues among a growing church. There were indifferences arising between the Greeks and Hebrews, widows in particular. The leaders of that day specifically the apostles realized they could not continue in their assignment to God and also meet the needs of a growing community of believers. This demand led them to identify able believers who could assist in ministering directly to the needs of the people while they continued in prayer and ministry of the word.

Today this truth is as equally important. Societies and churches are growing at a phenomenal rate and so are the needs of the people as was the case in Acts chapter 6. As leaders and ministry gifts establish a commitment to continual pray and study of the word others will be identified and positioned to minister to the daily needs of people. This is important because meeting the needs of people will give way to tremendous momentum and breakthrough for Kingdom advancement.

Kingdom Principle

37

Prayer helps us to strategically overcome ensuing threats of enemy siege.

It came to pass after this also, that the children of Moab, and the children of Ammon, and with them other beside the Ammonites, came against Jehoshaphat to battle. Then there came some that told Jehoshaphat saying, There cometh a great multitude against thee from beyond the sea on this side Syria; and behold, they be in Hazazon-tamar, which is En-gedi. And Jehoshaphat feared, and set himself to seek the Lord, and proclaimed a fast throughout all of Judah. And Judah gathered themselves together, to ask help of the Lord: even out of all of the cities of Judah they came to seek the Lord. And Jehoshaphat stood in the congregation of Judah and Jerusalem, in the house of the Lord, before the new court.

II Chronicles 20:1-5

King Jehoshaphat found himself confronted with a viable threat which was certain to destroy all of Judah. He takes evasive action after receiving reports concerning the great multiples according to II Chronicles 20:2. Jehoshaphat feared, set himself to seek the Lord and proclaimed a fast. (II Chronicles 20:3)

This was his strategic approach that would give way to divine intervene and Judah's deliverance. His prayed was the genesis of their enemies defeat, verse 4-12 is the actual prayer. In summary, it could be said that King Jehoshaphat lead all of Judah in corporate prayer asking God for help. He reminds God of previous victories that He preformed for His covenant people and then invokes a promise that God made to King Solomon in verse 9 *"If, when evil cometh upon us, as the sword, judgment, or pestilence, or famine, we stand before this house, and in thy presence, (for thy name is in this house,) and cry unto thee in our affliction, then thou wilt hear and help."* (see II Chronicles 6:28-30)

Upon the completion of their corporate prayer a prophet gives the next phase of the strategy to defeat the enemy. There are times during corporate prayer where the spirit of God will release supernatural insight to prophets and prophetic people who pray. In this case Jahaziel gets instruction to send singers and musicians to bow first. God fought through inspired praise and worship and the great multitude that was coming against Judah was overthrown and defeated in the wilderness. This victory also became a wealth transfer assignment according to verse 25. May this type of success be granted as you embrace the strategies of God to pray for Kingdom advancement.

Kingdom Principle

Prayer break generational and territorial influences rooted in unlawful actions.

¹Then there was a famine in the days of David three years, year after year; and King David enquired of the Lord. And the Lord answered, it is for Saul, and for his bloody house, because he slew the Gibeonites.

¹⁰ And Rizpah the daughter of Aiah took sackcloth, and spread it for her upon the rock, from the beginning of harvest until water dropped upon them out of heaven, and suffered neither the birds of the air to rest on them by day, nor the beasts of the field by night.

II Samuel 21:1 & 10

The nation of Israel is gripped by a famine for three (3) years. King David inquired the Lord, "Why the famine?" The Lord replies that the root cause of the famine was Saul and his bloody house because of what he did against the Gibeonites. They were a nation which came into covenant with Israel during the days of Joshua. They deceived the Israelites; and before the truth was revealed, a covenant was made securing them from destruction (see Joshua 9).

Rizaph, whose name means *hot stone*, lost two (2) sons; and Michal, Saul's daughter, lost five (5) sons. Their sons were hung by the Gibeonites as a means of restitution for the wickedness of Saul. This act occurred during the days of the harvest. Rizaph takes sackcloth and spreads it upon a rock. (Symbolically she humbles herself with fasting on a rock, which is prophetic of Christ our Rock.) She sets a watch by day, warding off the birds from eating the caucuses. And by night, she keeps away the beasts of the field. She positioned herself there from the beginning of harvest until water fell from heaven. *(source: Pray Without Ceasing A Guide to Effective Intercession)*

There presents several noteworthy acts that are viable today, for example sins that are taking place in any territory which are effecting the land and reducing the quality of life for its citizens is something that we are all acquainted with. In the context of urban communities, such as Chicago, Detroit, LA, or New York, gang violence is nothing new. From acts of murder, drug dealing, smuggling, extortion, etc innocent people suffer When leaders begin to inquire of God, "why is this happening in our land?", God will reveal the root causes and Rizaph type intercessors will be raised up to help break the seize of wickedness that is ravaging the lives of innocent citizens.

Kingdom Principle

39

Prayer challenges the believer practice forgiveness as a lifestyle.

For verily I say unto you that whosoever shall say unto this mountain be thou removed and be thou cast into the sea: and shall not doubt in his heart, but shall believe that those things which he said shall come to pass he shall have whatsoever he saith. Therefore I say unto whatsoever things ye desire when you pray believe that you receive them and you shall have them. And when you stand praying forgive if you have ought against any: that your Father also which is heaven may forgive you your trespasses. Mark 11:22-23

Our words are powerful in a sense that they can cause things to be removed or remain. In the context of Mark 11 what we say can literally cause mountains to be removed and tossed into the sea if we don't doubt, but believe the things we say will come to pass.

Now in the place of prayer we are encouraged to believe that whatever we pray for we receive. However, the underlining issue is always based on praying with a heart full of forgiveness. Many well to do intercessors and believers alike have found their life of prayer brought to a screeching halt because they don't forgive.

If you and I are to abide faithful and effective in our ministry assignment we must practice forgiving.

Kingdom Principle:

Prayer is the key that releases the believer to mature in the will of God.

Epaphras, who is one of you, a servant of Christ, saluteth you, always labouring fervently for you in prayers, that ye may stand perfect and complete in all the will of God.

Colossians 4:12

Epaphras represents the believer or the corporate body of believers who have a bent to see the body of Christ developed, established and mature in the will of God. His personal commitment to labour fervently in prayers was the means for the reality to take place in the church of Colosse. In this generation and those to come Epaphras type intercessors who prove to be of grave importance in helping the church mature and the kingdom of God advanced.

May the Kingdom principles of these pages stir you to become one who is relentless in prayer and passionately inspired to pray without ceasing.

More Great Resources from
Rivers of Living Water

Books

- Apostolic Pioneering
- Benefits of Praying in Tongues
- Exposing the Spirit of Anger
- Fundamentals of Deliverance 101, Revised and Expanded
- Ministering Spirits: "Engaging the Angelic Realm"
- Pray Without Ceasing, Special Edition
- Restoring Prophetic Watchmen
- Deliver Us From Evil
- Prayers, Decrees and Confessions for Wisdom
- Prayers, Decrees and Confessions for Favour and Grace
- Prayers, Decrees and Confessions for Prosperity
- Prayers, Decrees and Confessions for Increase
- Prayers, Decrees and Confessions for Righteousness, Revised & Expanded

CD's

- Prayers For The Nations
- Prayers Against Python &.Witchcraft
- Prayers Of Healing & Restoration
- Prayers of Renunciation and Deliverance
- Thy Kingdom Come
- The Glory
- Overcoming Spirits of Terrorism
- Songs of Intercession
- The Spirit of the Breaker

**Visit our online Ministry Bookstore at www.rolwchicago.com
or email: rolwfamily@yahoo.com**